BECOMING A PRO
HOCKEY
PLAYER

BY RYAN NAGELHOUT

Gareth Stevens
PUBLISHING

Please visit our website, www.garethstevens.com. For a free color catalog of all our high-quality books, call toll free 1-800-542-2595 or fax 1-877-542-2596.

Library of Congress Cataloging-in-Publication Data

Nagelhout, Ryan.
Becoming a pro hockey player / by Ryan Nagelhout.
p. cm. — (Going pro)
Includes index.
ISBN 978-1-4824-2066-1 (pbk.)
ISBN 978-1-4824-2065-4 (6-pack)
ISBN 978-1-4824-2067-8 (library binding)
1. Hockey — Juvenile literature. I. Nagelhout, Ryan. II. Title.
GV847.25 N34 2015
796.962 —d23

First Edition

Published in 2015 by
Gareth Stevens Publishing
111 East 14th Street, Suite 349
New York, NY 10003

Designer: Nicholas Domiano
Editor: Therese Shea

Photo credits: Cover, p. 1 peepo/Vetta/Getty Images; p. 5 (inset) David E. Klutho/Sports Illustrated/Getty Images; p. 5 (main) Kevork Djansezian/Getty Images Sport/Getty Images; p. 7 Thearon W. Henderson/ Getty Images Sport/Getty Images; p. 9 Lorraine Swanson/Shutterstock.com; p. 11 Bruce Bennett/Getty Images; p. 12 Marc Piscotty/Getty Images Sport/Getty Images; pp. 13, 17 Bruce Bennett/Getty Images Sport/Getty Images; p. 16 Len Redkoles/Nation Hockey League/Getty Images; p. 15 Dennis Pajot/Getty Images Sport/Getty Images; p. 19 Mitchell Layton/Getty Images Sport/Getty Images; p. 21 Scott Audette/ National Hockey League/Getty Images; p. 23 Abelimages/Getty Images Sport/Getty Images; p. 25 Andre Ringuette/National Hockey League/Getty Images; p. 26 B Bennett/Getty Images Sport/Getty Images; p. 27 Gregory Shamus/National Hockey League/Getty Images; p. 28 S Levy/Bruce Bennett/Getty Images; p. 29 (rink) Bardocz Peter/Shutterstock.com; p. 29 (players) Orion-v/Shutterstock.com; p. 29 (background) Shooter Bob Square Lenses/Shutterstock.com.

Printed in the United States of America

CPSIA compliance information: Batch #CW15GS: For further information contact Gareth Stevens, New York, New York at 1-800-542-2595.

CONTENTS

Words in the glossary appear in **bold** type the first time they are used in the text.

DREAMING OF THE CUP

The Stanley Cup weighs about 35 pounds (16 kg) and stands more than 35 inches (89 cm) tall. Given to the champions of the National Hockey League (NHL), the cup is almost as tall as the many children who dream of lifting the heavy prize over their head at the end of a long season.

Becoming a Stanley Cup champion is a long and hard process, but even making it to the NHL isn't easy. From first learning to skate to making a pro team, it takes years of hard work and **dedication** to make it as a pro hockey player.

COOLEST GAME ON ICE

There are many different kinds of hockey, such as field hockey and roller hockey. NHL games are played on ice, either outside in the cold or in a special building called a rink that keeps ice cold enough to stay frozen. No matter how you start playing hockey, the most famous pros all end up on ice.

In 2014, the Los Angeles Kings took home the Stanley Cup.

LEARNING TO SKATE

The first thing future pro hockey players need to do is learn how to skate. Ice hockey is different from other sports in that you can't just throw on sneakers and go play. You need to learn how to use ice skates, which are boots with sharp blades on the bottom. The blades glide on the ice when you push off.

Some kids learn to skate when they're just a few years old, but it's never too late to start! Many ice-skating rinks have learn-to-skate classes for all ages. Learning how to skate the right way can help you start your pro dreams!

CANADA'S GAME

Most people say hockey was invented in eastern Canada in the mid-1800s. In 1877, the first hockey team was formed at McGill University in Montreal, Québec. The Stanley Cup was first given out in 1893 to the Montreal **Amateur** Athletic Association. Today, millions of people play hockey all around the world.

Pro hockey players are more than just good ice-skaters—they're fast ice-skaters!

JOINING A TEAM

The next step for those who want to play hockey is to join a team! Playing at home is a great way to practice, but local youth teams and coaches help you learn the rules and how to play well with others.

Kids as young as 6 can play in some hockey leagues. USA Hockey has leagues in different age groups from 8 and under (Mite) to 18 and under (Midget) for youth hockey. Girls-only leagues run from 8-and-under leagues to age 19.

Coaches can help you and your parents figure out what league level is right for you and your skills.

A DANGEROUS GAME

All sports can be dangerous, including hockey. Every hockey player can get hurt on any play. Always make sure you wear proper safety **equipment** like helmets and pads when you play. It's also important to tell coaches and parents when you feel hurt, especially if it's your head that's bothering you.

Playing on a youth hockey team is the best way to learn the rules of hockey.

BUILDING SKILLS

As you get older and play more games, you'll learn your strengths as a player. You'll learn how to stop on ice and how to shoot the puck properly. Coaches will help you learn how to pass to teammates and teach you how to set up plays. You'll also pick a position to play.

Wayne Gretzky was one of the greatest hockey players of all time. He wasn't the fastest skater, but he learned to escape getting hit by other players and pass really well. These skills helped him play in leagues with players older than himself, which helped him improve more quickly.

CAMP BOUND

One way to build up your hockey skills is to attend camps held by coaches and players. Hockey camps are held all over the world. Some camps are held for certain positions, like goaltenders or defensemen, while others help you work on general hockey skills like shooting and passing. Hockey camps are usually held during the summer when most leagues don't play.

Wayne Gretzky started out playing youth hockey in his home country of Canada. He became a pro in 1978, playing for the Edmonton Oilers, the Los Angeles Kings, and the New York Rangers during his time in the NHL.

SCHOOL OR CLUB?

Many people play in a few different leagues. Travel hockey teams go all over the country to play against other travel clubs in **tournaments**. House leagues usually stay in the same rink and play other local teams.

Some schools have modified teams for middle school players, which sometimes have different rules to keep younger players safe. You can also try out for your high school's hockey team. Most schools have teams divided into two levels. Junior varsity teams are for younger, less skilled players. Varsity teams commonly have older and more skilled players. On these teams, you'll play teams from other schools nearby.

A GAME FOR EVERYONE

People who have major leg injuries or disabilities can play hockey, too! They play hockey sitting on special sleds with skate blades on the bottom of them. They use short sticks in each hand to shoot and push their sleds. Sled hockey players even have their own leagues.

ZACH BRANDON

SIDNEY CROSBY

Shattuck-Saint Mary's is a high school in Minnesota where NHL stars like Sidney Crosby and Nathan MacKinnon played before getting **drafted** first overall.

JUNIOR HOCKEY

The best youth hockey players end up playing junior hockey. The biggest leagues are in Canada and include the Ontario Hockey League (OHL), Québec Major Junior Hockey League (QMJHL), and the Western Hockey League (WHL). Players ages 16 to 20 are allowed to play junior hockey.

The top junior hockey league in the United States is the United States Hockey League (USHL). With teams around the country, many junior hockey players end up moving away from their family. They stay with **billet** families who take these players in, make sure they go to school, and give them a home away from home.

WORLDWIDE COMPETITION

The competition in junior hockey is tough, but it's even tougher in the World Juniors held each year by the International Ice Hockey Federation (IIHF). Different countries make teams of promising players under 20 years old and play one another. Playing well in the World Juniors can really help a player who's hoping to get drafted turn heads.

Junior hockey is where most NHL scouts start looking for players to draft.

THE COLLEGE PATH

After you're done with high school, you can play college hockey. There are different divisions in NCAA (National Collegiate Athletic Association) college hockey, but Division I has the biggest schools and best players. Most of these schools offer **scholarships** to players who choose to attend school there. Schools like the University of Minnesota and University of North Dakota have very respected hockey programs. The best teams compete in a tournament at the end of the season called the Frozen Four.

College hockey is becoming a more popular path to the NHL in recent years. Minnesota Wild star Zach Parise and Los Angeles Kings goaltender Jonathan Quick are two NHL stars who played college hockey.

UNDER DEVELOPMENT

Some of the best young hockey players in the country work with USA Hockey's National Team Development Program. Started in 1996 in Ann Arbor, Michigan, the program helps get players ready for World Juniors tournaments and later the NHL. A number of future NHL stars have played on this team, including Chicago Blackhawks superstar Patrick Kane.

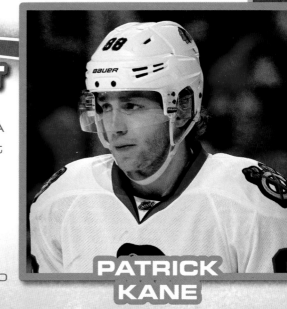

PATRICK KANE

Zach Parise (number 9) played for the University of North Dakota before the New Jersey Devils drafted him in 2003. He also played for Team USA at the 2014 Olympic Games!

HITTING THE LOTTERY

Each summer, the NHL holds a draft to pick future players. This is how most hockey players get the chance to go pro. The draft is seven rounds, with all the NHL teams getting a pick in each round. Players must be at least 19 years old to enter the draft, though certain NHL rules allow some players to enter at age 18, too.

A few weeks before the draft, the league holds a **combine**. Scouts from each team attend the combine, watch films of players' games, and ask players questions to see if they're a good fit for a team.

PROSPECT CAMP

After the draft, many teams hold a prospect or development camp. They invite their drafted players and other young players not on an NHL roster, or team list, to go through drills and get to know the team's coaches. A good showing at prospect camp can help players make the team!

Washington Capitals player Alex Ovechkin was the first overall pick in the 2004 NHL Draft.

WHAT'S NEXT?

Now that you're drafted, what happens next? Usually the answer is simple: nothing. Because draft picks are so young, most players just go back to their college or junior teams. Only a few players—usually just the top pick—go right to the NHL that fall! Playing well wherever you are is important when you're both a prospect and a drafted player. NHL teams want to see players improve.

When an NHL team is ready to bring a draft pick in to play for them, the prospect signs an entry-level contract. This includes a player taking the ice for the team's minor league **affiliate**.

MISSING THE CUT

Your NHL dreams aren't over just because you didn't get drafted! College players that go undrafted and keep at it can finish their time at school and still sign with an NHL team. Many will have more than 1 year of draft **eligibility**, so they can try again next season!

Tampa Bay Lightning forward Steven Stamkos is one of the few NHL players to get drafted and play in the NHL a few months later. He was the first overall draft pick in 2008.

THE MINOR LEAGUES

Going from prospect to pro is usually a long process for hockey players. Even after being drafted, players may continue playing in college or juniors for years! Then, once they sign a contract with an NHL team, they still don't suit up right away. Many play in the minor leagues on teams like the Rochester Americans or Hamilton Bulldogs of the American Hockey League (AHL).

On the roster of AHL affiliates, at least 13 players must be considered "development" players. The AHL is meant to help young hockey players get ready for a career in the NHL.

THE GAP

AHL prospects must be 18 years old by September 15 of the year they would start playing. However, players drafted by NHL teams from junior hockey teams can't join the AHL until they are 20 or have played 4 years of junior hockey. So, some drafted junior players have to play on junior hockey teams for an extra season before playing in the AHL.

The Rochester Americans are the AHL affiliate for the NHL's Buffalo Sabres.

TRAINING CAMP

Every September, all the NHL teams gather to get ready for the start of another season. Teams invite many of their prospects and other players under contract to practice and try to make the team's 23-player roster. For dozens of prospects, this is their chance to finally make a pro hockey team.

Making the opening night roster doesn't mean you're a pro for good. If you don't play well in the NHL, you could get sent back down to the minors. Many young players have options in their contracts that let a team send them down to the minors a number of times.

OTHER LEAGUES

The NHL is considered the best, but there are many other pro leagues around the world. Germany, Sweden, and Finland each have a pro league filled with great hockey players. The Kontinental Hockey League (KHL) is a popular pro hockey league in Russia and other European countries that started in 2008.

Some players bounce back and forth between NHL and minor league clubs many times. This image shows Mika Zibanejad when he was called up from the AHL to play for the Ottawa Senators in January 2013.

TRADES, WAIVERS, AND FREE AGENCY

Signing a contract with a team doesn't mean you play there your entire career. Many players are traded between teams. This happens if the player doesn't fit a team's style or doesn't play well. One player may be traded for another or even for more than one player! Another way players move between teams is being put on **waiver**.

Once your entry-level contract is up, you can sign a new one with the team that drafted you. After your second contract, though, you're a free agent. You can sign with any team you want!

WOMEN IN HOCKEY

Only one woman has ever played NHL hockey. In 1992, goaltender Manon Rhéaume played in two exhibition games for the Tampa Bay Lightning. No woman has played in the league since. There are few women's pro hockey leagues, but the Canadian Women's Hockey League (CWHL) has seen some growth.

MANON RHÉAUME

More than half of players in the NHL play fewer than six seasons—and fewer than 100 games.

WINNING IT ALL

Only one team gets to lift the Stanley Cup at the end of a long season. Being lucky enough to play on that team means your name goes on the cup! You also get to spend a day with the big silver trophy. Many players bring the cup home with them! Some even take it to the billet families that helped them through junior hockey and the draft.

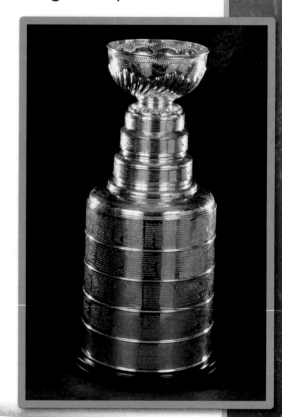

After years of hard work, many hockey players share their victory with the people who helped make their dreams a reality. With the help of so many people, they made it to the pros. Now it's time to celebrate!

ONLY A GAME

With all the hockey camps and leagues out there, it's important to remember that hockey is supposed to be fun. No one is an NHL superstar when they're in elementary school. It takes years to figure out who can go pro. So go out there and just have fun!

HOCKEY POSITIONS

goalie

defenseman   defenseman

right wing   center   left wing

left wing   center   right wing

defenseman   defenseman

goalie

GLOSSARY

affiliate: a closely connected team

amateur: someone who does something without pay

billet: an assigned home for a junior hockey player

combine: an event that brings players together to test their skills

dedication: commitment

draft: to select a player from a pool of potential players entering the league. Also, the process of selecting new players.

eligibility: the amount of time you are allowed to play in college or get drafted

equipment: tools, clothing, and other items needed for a job

scholarship: money awarded to a student to pay for their college education

tournament: a series of contests testing the skill of many athletes in the same sport

waiver: the act of allowing another team to claim a player and his contract

FOR MORE INFORMATION

Books

Hawkins, Jeff. *Playing Pro Hockey.* Minneapolis, MN: Lerner Publications, 2015.

Savage, Jeff. *Super Hockey Infographics.* Minneapolis, MN: Lerner Publications, 2015.

Storden, Thom. *Amazing Hockey Records.* North Mankato, MN: Capstone Press, 2015.

Websites

Hockey Reference
hockey-reference.com
Visit this site to find statistics for your favorite players and team.

Hockey's Future
hockeysfuture.com
Learn about the stars of tomorrow on this prospect site.

The Official Site of the NHL
nhl.com
Find schedules and more information about the National Hockey League here.

Publisher's note to educators and parents: Our editors have carefully reviewed these websites to ensure that they are suitable for students. Many websites change frequently, however, and we cannot guarantee that a site's future contents will continue to meet our high standards of quality and educational value. Be advised that students should be closely supervised whenever they access the Internet.

INDEX